MELODY, GUITAR CHORDS AND FULL LYRICS

TIME OUT OF MIND
BOB DYLAN

MELODY, GUITAR CHORDS AND FULL LYRICS

TIME OUT OF MIND
BOB DYLAN

WISE PUBLICATIONS
PART OF THE MUSIC SALES GROUP
LONDON / NEW YORK / PARIS / SYDNEY / COPENHAGEN / BERLIN / MADRID / HONG KONG / TOKYO

INTRODUCTION

The 1997 'comeback' album *Time Out Of Mind* represents a bright highlight in the career of Bob Dylan, and not merely because this was the first album of original material since *Under The Red Sky* in 1990. The substance of this triple-Grammy Award winning release paints a portrait of an artist now archiving his own work; of a man becoming aware of his own mortality; and of a pioneer still urgently seeking and discovering.

These perspectives are perhaps most clearly heard together on the pivotal 'Not Dark Yet', the beating heart of the album:

Shadows are falling and I've been here all day
It's too hot to sleep, time is running away
Feel like my soul has turned into steel
I've still got the scars that the sun didn't heal
There's not even room enough to be anywhere
It's not dark yet, but it's getting there

Despite the sophisticated 10-beat metre and the ephemeral, Daniel Lanois-produced guitar swells, there is a natural simplicity even here that frames it within the American folk tradition.

Indeed, apart from the twin ballads with their endlessly descending bass lines, 'Standing In The Doorway' and 'Make You Feel My Love', almost every song on the album is in fact a blues—either directly in form and style ('Dirt Road Blues', 'Million Miles', 'Till I Fell In Love With You', 'Can't Wait' and the 16-minute epic 'Highlands') or else in terms of the interwoven harmonic, melodic and tonal language ('Love Sick' and 'Cold Irons Bound').

The genre emerges as the perfect vehicle for this late-career confessional. The immediate simplicity and emotional transparency of the form are not new to Dylan, of course: every one of his early albums contains at least one blues song. Indeed, the two albums prior to this one—*Good As I Been To You* and *World Gone Wrong*—are collections of traditional music including folk-blues songs, but *Time Out Of Mind* is the first album to explore the blues in such overt depth.

In Dylan's memoirs, *Chronicles: Volume One*, he recounts how, soon after arriving in New York City, he began hanging out at the Folklore Center where he immersed himself in American music. He details Izzy Young, the owner, playing him a bluegrass standard from the *Anthology*:

'He played me "White House Blues" by Charlie Poole and said that this would be perfect for me and pointed out that this was the exact version that The Ramblers did.'

Bob Dylan, *Chronicles: Volume One*

He later tells of his first encounter with the songs of Robert Johnson in Dave van Ronk's apartment:

'I had the thick acetate of the Robert Johnson record in my hands and I asked Van Ronk if he ever heard of him. Dave said, nope, he hadn't, and I put it on the record player so we could listen to it. From the first note the vibrations from the loudspeaker made my hair stand up. The stabbing sounds from the guitar could almost break a window. When Johnson started singing, he seemed like a guy who could have sprung from the head of Zeus in full armor. I immediately differentiated between him and anyone else I had ever heard. The songs weren't customary blues songs. They were perfected pieces—each song contained four or five verses, every couplet intertwined with the next but in no obvious way. They were so utterly fluid. At first they went by quick, too quick to even get. They jumped all over the place in range and subject matter, short punchy verses that resulted in some panoramic story—fires of mankind blasting off the surface of this spinning piece of plastic.'

Bob Dylan, *Chronicles: Volume One*

Certainly, the earthy excitement of the blues, together with the uncomplicated, natural sound of early gramophone recordings, contributed hugely to the overall recording process of *Time Out Of Mind*.

Time Out Of Mind closes with the longest Dylan song on record, 'Highlands'. Beneath the entire song rolls a repeating riff on two guitars evidently inspired by early bluesman Charley Patton. This endless loop frames the nature of time itself: relentless, continuous, enduring. You could try this single-guitar version instead of the simpler picking pattern written in the music:

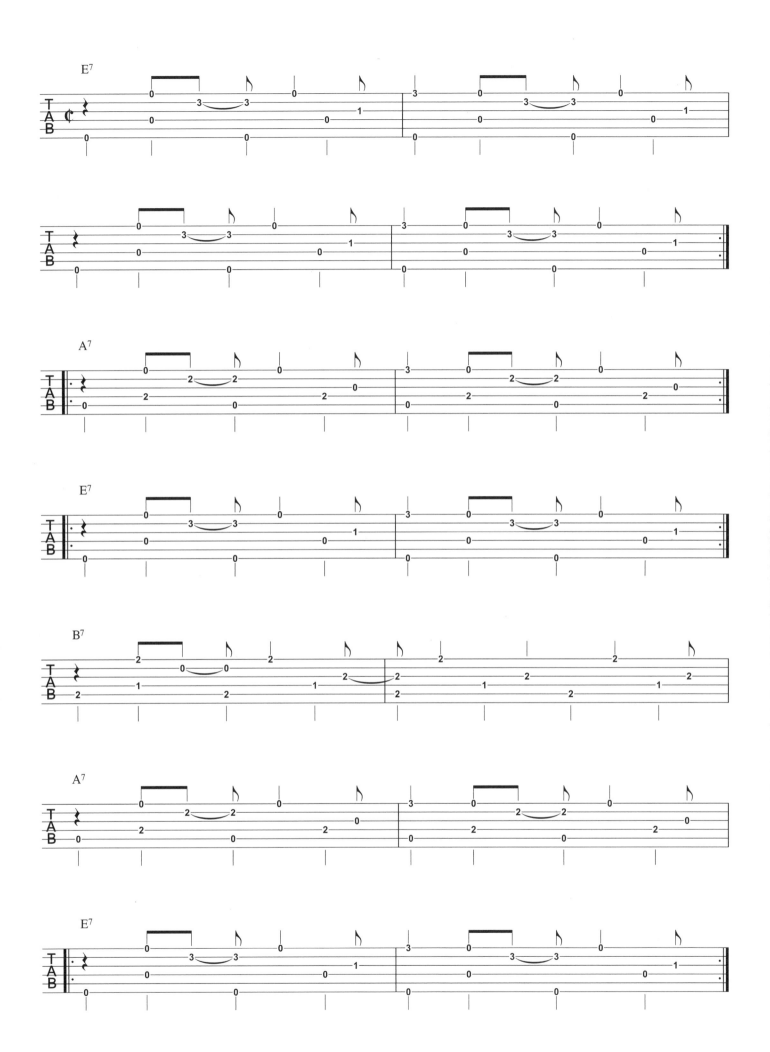

LOVE SICK

WORDS AND MUSIC BY BOB DYLAN

Strumming style:

Verse ♩ = 70

1. I'm walk-ing through streets that are__ dead.__
2. Did I hear some - one__ tell a lie?____

Walk - ing, walk - ing__ with you__ in my head.__
Did I hear some - one's dis - tant

cry? My feet are so tired, my brain is so wired__
You thrilled me to my heart, then you ripped it all a - part, you went through my pock -

1. and the clouds__ are weep-ing.__

- ets when I was

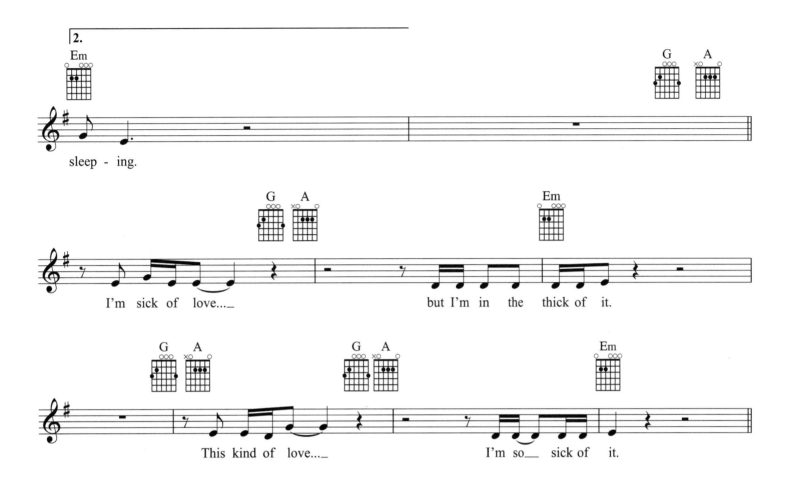

Verse 3

I see lovers in the meadow
I see silhouettes in the window
I watch them 'til they're gone and they leave me hanging on
To a shadow

I'm sick of love... I hear the clock tick
I'm sick of love... I'm love sick

Verse 4

Sometimes the silence can be like the thunder
Sometimes I feel like I'm being plowed under
Could you ever be true? I think of you
And I wonder

I'm sick of love... I wish I'd never met you
I'm sick of love... I'm trying to forget you

Just don't know what to do
I'd give anything to just be with you

9

DIRT ROAD BLUES

WORDS AND MUSIC BY BOB DYLAN

Strumming style:

Gon' walk down_ that dirt road, 'til some-one lets me ride._

Gon' walk down_ that dirt road, 'til some-one lets me ride._

If I can't find my ba-by,_

I'm gon-na run a-way_ and hide._

10

Verse 2

I been pacing around the room hoping maybe she'd come back
Pacing 'round the room hoping maybe she'd come back
Well, I been praying for salvation laying 'round in a one-room country shack

Verse 3

Gon' walk down that dirt road until my eyes begin to bleed
Gon' walk down that dirt road until my eyes begin to bleed
'Til there's nothing left to see, 'til the chains have been shattered and I've been freed

Verse 4

I been lookin' at my shadow, I been watching the colors up above
Lookin' at my shadow, watching the colors up above
Rolling through the rain and hail, looking for the sunny side of love

Verse 5

Gon' walk on down that dirt road 'til I'm right beside the sun
Gon' walk on down until I'm right beside the sun
I'm gonna have to put up a barrier to keep myself away from everyone

MILLION MILES

WORDS AND MUSIC BY BOB DYLAN

Capo: 4th fret
Strumming style:

(Swing)

You took a part of me that I_____ real-ly miss,___

I keep ask-ing my-self how long it can go on like this. You

told your-self a lie,___ that's all right ma-ma I told my-self one too.___

___ I'm tryin'___ to get clos-er but I'm

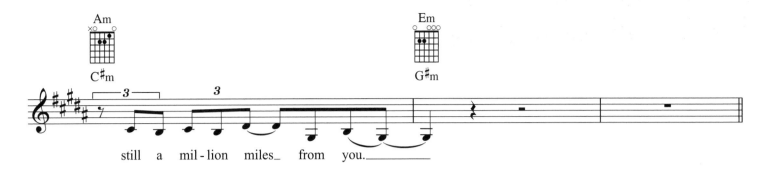

still   a   mil - lion   miles_   from   you._____

Verse 2

You took the silver, you took the gold
You left me standing out in the cold
People asked about you, I didn't tell them everything I knew
Well, I'm tryin' to get closer but I'm still a million miles from you

Verse 3

I'm drifting in and out of dreamless sleep
Throwing all my memories in a ditch so deep
Did so many things I never did intend to do
Well, I'm tryin' to get closer but I'm still a million miles from you

Verse 4

I need your love so bad, turn your lamp down low
I need every bit of it for the places that I go
Sometimes I wonder just what it's all coming to
Well, I'm tryin' to get closer but I'm still a million miles from you

Verse 5

Well, I don't dare close my eyes and I don't dare wink
Maybe in the next life I'll be able to hear myself think
Feel like talking to somebody but I just don't know who
Well, I'm tryin' to get closer but I'm still a million miles from you

Verse 6

The last thing you said before you hit the street
"Gonna find me a janitor to sweep me off my feet"
I said, "That's all right, you do what you gotta do"
Well, I'm tryin' to get closer, I'm still a million miles from you

Verse 7

Rock me, pretty baby, rock me 'til everything gets real
Rock me for a little while, rock me 'til there's nothing left to feel
And I'll rock you too
I'm tryin' to get closer but I'm still a million miles from you

Verse 8

Well, there's voices in the night trying to be heard
I'm sitting here listening to every mind-polluting word
I know plenty of people who would put me up for a day or two
Yes, I'm tryin' to get closer but I'm still a million miles from you

STANDING IN THE DOORWAY

WORDS AND MUSIC BY BOB DYLAN

Capo: 4th fret
Picking style:

♩ = 66

Verse

1. I'm walk-ing through the sum-mer nights, juke-box play-ing low.

Yes-ter-day ev-'ry-thing was go-ing too fast,

to - day, it's mov-ing too slow.

14

Verse 2

The light in this place is so bad
Making me sick in the head
All the laughter is just making me sad
The stars have turned cherry red
I'm strumming on my gay guitar
Smoking a cheap cigar
The ghost of our old love has not gone away
Don't look like it will anytime soon
You left me standing in the doorway crying
Under the midnight moon

Verse 3

Maybe they'll get me and maybe they won't
But not tonight and it won't be here
There are things I could say but I don't
I know the mercy of God must be near
I've been riding the midnight train
Got ice water in my veins
I would be crazy if I took you back
It would go up against every rule
You left me standing in the doorway crying
Suffering like a fool

Verse 4

When the last rays of daylight go down
Buddy, you'll roll no more
I can hear the church bells ringing in the yard
I wonder who they're ringing for
I know I can't win
But my heart just won't give in
Last night I danced with a stranger
But she just reminded me you were the one
You left me standing in the doorway crying
In the dark land of the sun

Verse 5

I'll eat when I'm hungry, drink when I'm dry
And live my life on the square
And even if the flesh falls off of my face
I know someone will be there to care
It always means so much
Even the softest touch
I see nothing to be gained by any explanation
There are no words that need to be said
You left me standing in the doorway crying
Blues wrapped around my head

TRYIN' TO GET TO HEAVEN

WORDS AND MUSIC BY BOB DYLAN

Capo: 3rd fret
Strumming style:

(heavy backbeat)

♩ = 92

Verse

The air is get-ting hot-ter,___ there's a rum-bl-ing in the skies..

___ I've been wad-ing through the high__ mud-dy wat-er

Verse 2

When I was in Missouri
They would not let me be
I had to leave there in a hurry
I only saw what they let me see
You broke a heart that loved you
Now you can seal up the book and not write anymore
I've been walking that lonesome valley
Trying to get to heaven before they close the door

Verse 3

People on the platforms
Waiting for the trains
I can hear their hearts a-beatin'
Like pendulums swinging on chains
I tried to give you everything
That your heart was longing for
I'm just going down the road feeling bad
Trying to get to heaven before they close the door

Verse 4

I'm going down the river
Down to New Orleans
They tell me everything is gonna be all right
But I don't know what "all right" even means
I was riding in a buggy with Miss Mary-Jane
Miss Mary-Jane got a house in Baltimore
I been all around the world, boys
Now I'm trying to get to heaven before they close the door

Verse 5

Gonna sleep down in the parlor
And relive my dreams
I'll close my eyes and I wonder
If everything is as hollow as it seems
When you think that you've lost everything
You find out you can always lose a little more
I been to Sugar Town, I shook the sugar down
Now I'm trying to get to heaven before they close the door

'TIL I FELL IN LOVE WITH YOU

WORDS AND MUSIC BY BOB DYLAN

Capo: 6th fret
Strumming style:

(shuffle)

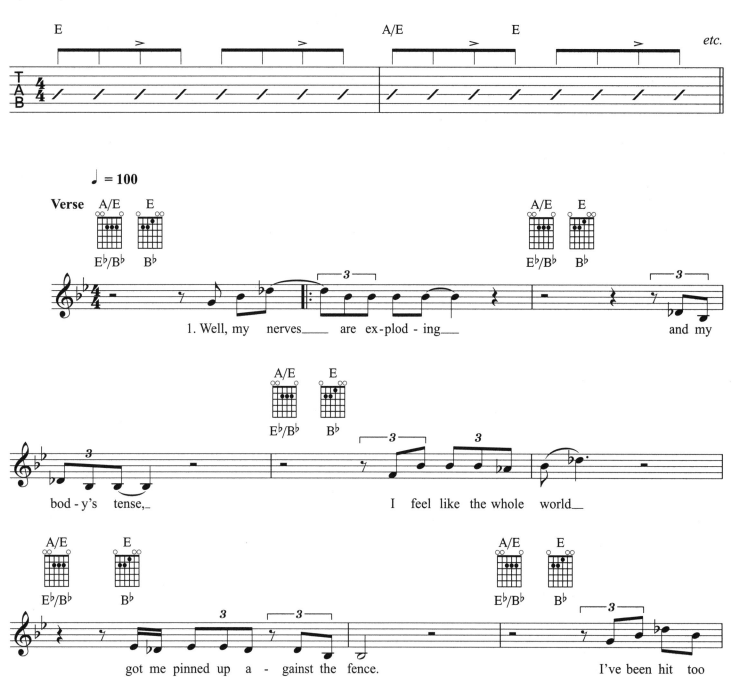

1. Well, my nerves___ are ex-plod-ing___ and my bod-y's tense,___ I feel like the whole world___ got me pinned up a-gainst the fence. I've been hit too

Verse 2

Well, my house is on fire, burning to the sky
I thought it would rain but the clouds passed by
Now I feel like I'm coming to the end of my way
But I know God is my shield and he won't lead me astray
Still I don't know what I'm gonna do
I was all right 'til I fell in love with you

Verse 3

Boys in the street beginning to play
Girls like birds flying away
When I'm gone you will remember my name
I'm gonna win my way to wealth and fame
I don't know what I'm gonna do
I was all right 'til I fell in love with you

Verse 4

Junk is piling up, taking up space
My eyes feel like they're falling off my face
Sweat falling down, I'm staring at the floor
I'm thinking about that girl who won't be back no more
I don't know what I'm gonna do
I was all right 'til I fell in love with you

Verse 5

Well, I'm tired of talking, I'm tired of trying to explain
My attempts to please you were all in vain
Tomorrow night before the sun goes down
If I'm still among the living, I'll be Dixie bound
I just don't know what I'm gonna do
I was all right 'til I fell in love with you

NOT DARK YET

WORDS AND MUSIC BY BOB DYLAN

Capo: 4th fret
Strumming style:

Verse

Sha - dows are fall - ing   and I've been here all day. —

— It's too hot to sleep, —

time is run - ning a - way. —

23

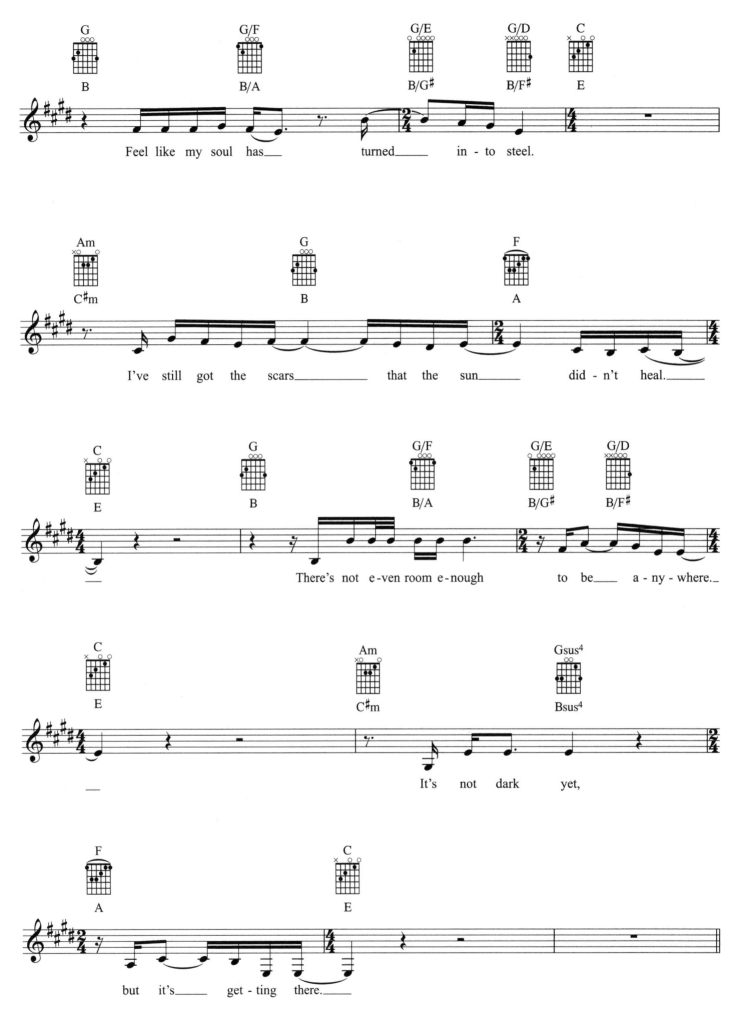

Verse 2

Well, my sense of humanity has gone down the drain
Behind every beautiful thing there's been some kind of pain
She wrote me a letter and she wrote it so kind
She put down in writing what was in her mind
I just don't see why I should even care
It's not dark yet, but it's getting there

Verse 3

Well, I've been to London and I've been to gay Paree
I've followed the river and I got to the sea
I've been down on the bottom of a world full of lies
I ain't looking for nothing in anyone's eyes
Sometimes my burden seems more than I can bear
It's not dark yet, but it's getting there

Verse 4

I was born here and I'll die here against my will
I know it looks like I'm moving, but I'm standing still
Every nerve in my body is so vacant and numb
I can't even remember what it was I came here to get away from
Don't even hear a murmur of a prayer
It's not dark yet, but it's getting there

COLD IRONS BOUND

WORDS AND MUSIC BY BOB DYLAN

Capo: 1st fret
Guitar riff:

I'm beg-in - ning to hear voi-ces and there's no-one a - round.___ Well, I'm

all used up___ and the fields have turned brown.___ I went to

church on Sun - day___ and she___ passed by,___ my love

for her_____ is tak - ing such a long__ time to___ die. I'm

Chorus

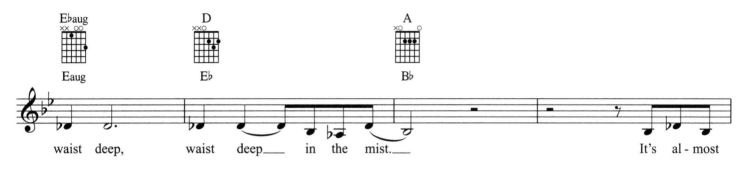

waist deep, waist deep___ in the mist.___ It's al - most

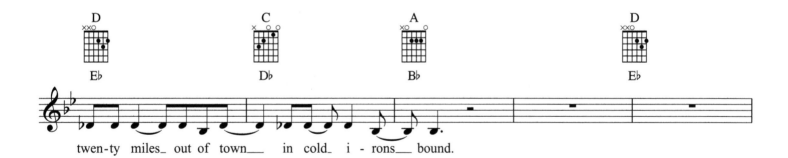

like, al - most like___ I don't ex - ist.___ I'm

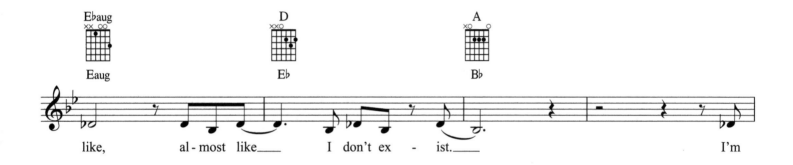

twen-ty miles_ out of town___ in cold_ i - rons_ bound.

2. The walls_

Verse 2

The walls of pride are high and wide
Can't see over to the other side
It's such a sad thing to see beauty decay
It's sadder still to feel your heart torn away

Chorus 2

One look at you and I'm out of control
Like the universe has swallowed me whole
I'm twenty miles out of town in cold irons bound

Verse 3

There's too many people, too many to recall
I thought some of 'm were friends of mine, I was wrong about 'm all
Well, the road is rocky and the hillside's mud
Up over my head nothing but clouds of blood

Chorus 3

I found my world, found my world in you
But your love just hasn't proved true
I'm twenty miles out of town in cold irons bound
Twenty miles out of town in cold irons bound

Verse 4

Oh, the winds in Chicago have torn me to shreds
Reality has always had too many heads
Some things last longer than you think they will
There are some kind of things you can never kill

Chorus 4

It's you and you only I been thinking about
But you can't see in and it's hard lookin' out
I'm twenty miles out of town in cold irons bound

Verse 5

Well the fat's in the fire and the water's in the tank
The whiskey's in the jar and the money's in the bank
I tried to love and protect you because I cared
I'm gonna remember forever the joy that we shared

Chorus 5

Looking at you and I'm on my bended knee
You have no idea what you do to me
I'm twenty miles out of town in cold irons bound
Twenty miles out of town in cold irons bound

MAKE YOU FEEL MY LOVE

WORDS AND MUSIC BY BOB DYLAN

Capo: 1st fret
Picking style:

29

When the eve - ning sha - dows and the stars___ ap - pear,___
(instrumental on repeat)

and there is no one there to dry___ your_ tears,___ I could hold you for a mil -

- lion years, to make you feel my love.___

Chorus

I know you have - n't made your mind up___ yet,___
The storms are rag - ing on the roll - in'___ sea,___

but I would nev - er do you wrong.___
and on the high - way of re - gret.___

HIGHLANDS

WORDS AND MUSIC BY BOB DYLAN

Picking style:

Well my heart's in the High-lands, gen-tle and fair, hon-ey-suc-kle bloom-ing in the wild-wood air,___ blue-bells blaz - ing where the Ab - er - deen wat - ers flow.

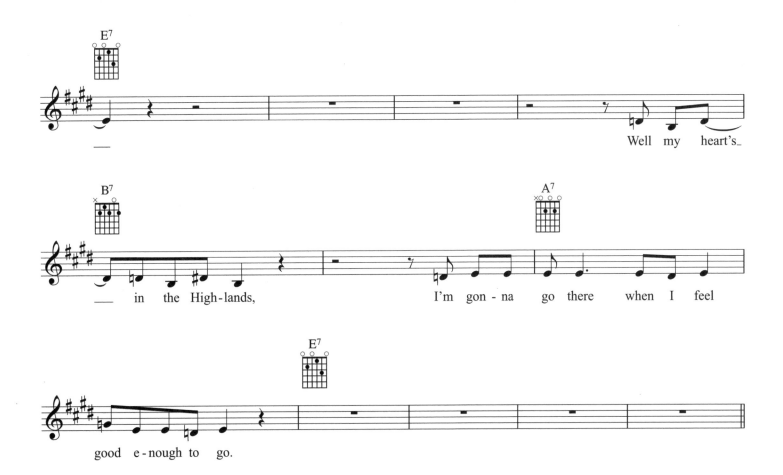

Well my heart's_ ___ in the High-lands, I'm gon - na go there when I feel good e - nough to go.

Verse 2

Windows were shakin' all night in my dreams
Everything was exactly the way that it seems
Woke up this morning and I looked at the same old page
Same ol' rat race
Life in the same ol' cage

Verse 3

I don't want nothing from anyone, ain't that much to take
Wouldn't know the difference between a real blonde and a fake
Feel like a prisoner in a world of mystery
I wish someone would come
And push back the clock for me

Verse 4

Well my heart's in the Highlands wherever I roam
That's where I'll be when I get called home
The wind, it whispers to the buck-eyed trees in rhyme
Well my heart's in the Highlands
I can only get there one step at a time

Verse 5

I'm listening to Neil Young, I gotta turn up the sound
Someone's always yelling turn it down
Feel like I'm drifting
Drifting from scene to scene
I'm wondering what in the devil could it all possibly mean?

Verse 6

Insanity is smashing up against my soul
You can say I was on anything but a roll
If I had a conscience, well, I just might blow my top
What would I do with it anyway
Maybe take it to the pawn shop

Verse 7

My heart's in the Highlands at the break of dawn
By the beautiful lake of the Black Swan
Big white clouds like chariots that swing down low
Well my heart's in the Highlands
Only place left to go

33

Verse 8
I'm in Boston town, in some restaurant
I got no idea what I want
Well, maybe I do but I'm just really not sure
Waitress comes over
Nobody in the place but me and her

Verse 9
It must be a holiday, there's nobody around
She studies me closely as I sit down
She got a pretty face and long white shiny legs
She says, "What'll it be?"
I say, "I don't know, you got any soft boiled eggs?"

Verse 10
She looks at me, says, "I'd bring you some
But we're out of 'm, you picked the wrong time to come"
Then she says, "I know you're an artist, draw a picture of me!"
I say, "I would if I could, but
I don't do sketches from memory"

Verse 11
"Well," she says, "I'm right here in front of you, or haven't you looked?"
I say, "All right, I know, but I don't have my drawing book!"
She gives me a napkin, she says, "You can do it on that"
I say, "Yes I could, but
I don't know where my pencil is at!"

Verse 12
She pulls one out from behind her ear
She says, "All right now, go ahead, draw me, I'm standing right here"
I make a few lines and I show it for her to see
Well she takes the napkin and throws it back
And says, "That don't look a thing like me!"

Verse 13
I said, "Oh, kind Miss, it most certainly does"
She says, "You must be jokin'." I say, "I wish I was!"
Then she says, "You don't read women authors, do you?"
Least that's what I think I hear her say
"Well," I say, "how would you know and what would it matter anyway?"

Verse 14
"Well," she says, "you just don't seem like you do!"
I said, "You're way wrong"
She says, "Which ones have you read then?" I say, "I read Erica Jong!"
She goes away for a minute
And I slide up out of my chair
I step outside back to the busy street but nobody's going anywhere

Verse 15

Well my heart's in the Highlands with the horses and hounds
Way up in the border country, far from the towns
With the twang of the arrow and a snap of the bow
My heart's in the Highlands
Can't see any other way to go

Verse 16

Every day is the same thing out the door
Feel further away than ever before
Some things in life, it gets too late to learn
Well, I'm lost somewhere
I must have made a few bad turns

Verse 17

I see people in the park forgetting their troubles and woes
They're drinking and dancing, wearing bright-colored clothes
All the young men with their young women looking so good
Well, I'd trade places with any of them
In a minute, if I could

Verse 18

I'm crossing the street to get away from a mangy dog
Talking to myself in a monologue
I think what I need might be a full-length leather coat
Somebody just asked me
If I registered to vote

Verse 19

The sun is beginning to shine on me
But it's not like the sun that used to be
The party's over and there's less and less to say
I got new eyes
Everything looks far away

Verse 20

Well, my heart's in the Highlands at the break of day
Over the hills and far away
There's a way to get there and I'll figure it out somehow
But I'm already there in my mind
And that's good enough for now

CAN'T WAIT

WORDS AND MUSIC BY BOB DYLAN

Capo: 4th fret
Strumming style:

(heavy backbeat)

I can't wait, wait for you to change your

mind. It's late, I'm trying to walk the

line. Well, it's way past mid-night and there are

peo-ple all a-round, some on their way up, some on their way down.

The air burns__ and I'm trying__ to think__ straight,__

and I__ don't know__ how much long-er I__ can wait.__

1, 2, 4.

3.

2. I'm your

I'm doomed to

Bridge

love you, I've been roll - ing through__ storm - y

wea - ther. I'm think-ing of you

D.S.

and all the plac - es we could roam to - geth - er. It's might - y

37

Verse 2

I'm your man, I'm trying to recover the sweet love that we knew
You understand that my heart can't go on beating without you
Well, your loveliness has wounded me, I'm reeling from the blow
I wish I knew what it was keeps me loving you so
I'm breathing hard, standing at the gate
But I don't know how much longer I can wait

Verse 3

Skies are grey, I'm looking for anything that will bring a happy glow
Night or day, it doesn't matter where I go anymore, I just go
If I ever saw you coming I don't know what I would do
I'd like to think I could control myself, but it isn't true
That's how it is when things disintegrate
And I don't know how much longer I can wait

Bridge

I'm doomed to love you, I've been rolling through stormy weather
I'm thinking of you and all the places we could roam together

Verse 4

It's mighty funny, the end of time has just begun
Oh, honey, after all these years you're still the one
While I'm strolling through the lonely graveyard of my mind
I left my life with you somewhere back there along the line
I thought somehow that I would be spared this fate
But I don't know how much longer I can wait

COLLECT THE SERIES...

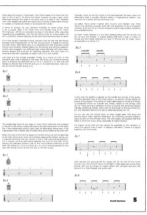

ORDER NO. AM1012946

ORDER NO. AM1012957